nh

Notting Hill Editions is an independent British publisher. The company was founded by Tom Kremer (1930–2017), champion of innovation and the man responsible for popularising the Rubik's Cube.

After a successful business career in toy invention Tom decided, at the age of eighty, to fulfil his passion for literature. In a fast-moving digital world Tom's aim was to revive the art of the essay, and to create exceptionally beautiful books that would be cherished.

Hailed as 'the shape of things to come', the family-run press brings to print the most surprising thinkers of past and present. In an era of information-overload, these collectible pocket-size books distil ideas that linger in the mind.

Charles Lutwidge Dodgson (1832–1898), better known as Lewis Carroll, was an English author, poet, mathematician, illustrator, photographer, inventor and insomniac. Most famous for writing *Alice's Adventures in Wonderland* (1865) and its sequel *Through the Looking-Glass* (1871), he was also noted for his love of puzzles and wordplay – the entertainments that feature in *Lewis Carroll's Guide for Insomniacs*. In 1856 Dodgson published his first work under the name that would make him famous when a romantic poem called 'Solitude' appeared in *The Train* under the authorship of 'Lewis Carroll'. The pen name was a play on his real name and translated into Latin as 'Carolus Ludovicus' and then translated back into English as 'Carroll Lewis' and reversed to make 'Lewis Carroll'. Dodgson's editor chose the name from a list of four submitted by Dodgson, the others being Edgar U. C. Westhill, Louis Carroll and Edgar Cuthwellis.

Phiz was the pen name of one of the greatest Victorian illustrators, Hablot Knight Browne (1815–1882), best known for illustrating the works of Charles Dickens. Phuz is the pen name of one of his alleged descendants, the noted contemporary artist, illustrator and maze-maker, David Farris.

Gyles Brandreth is a writer, broadcaster, performer, former MP and Lord Commissioner of the Treasury, now Chancellor of the University of Chester, who has been a devotee of Lewis Carroll since he saw a production of *Through the Looking-Glass* when he was seven. In the 1970s he created a one-man Lewis Carroll stage show and TV series for the entertainer Cyril Fletcher. In the 1980s he devised the *Alice in Wonderland* board game for the makers of Scrabble. More recently, with Susannah Pearse, he created the musical *Wonderland* about Charles Dodgson and his friendship with the actress Isa Bowman. In 2023, with descendants of the Dodgson family and the great-grandchildren of Alice Liddell (the original Alice), he unveiled a plaque at Folly Bridge in Oxford, on the bank of the river Isis, commemorating the boat trip that took place on 'the golden afternoon' of 4 July 1862 when the story of Alice's adventures was told for the first time.

LEWIS CARROLL'S GUIDE
FOR INSOMNIACS

–

Introduced by
Gyles Brandreth

Edited by
Edgar Cuthwellis

Illustrations by
Phuz

nh Notting Hill Editions

First published in 1979 by J. M. Dent & Sons Ltd

Published in 2024
by Notting Hill Editions Ltd
Mirefoot, Burneside, Kendal LA8 9AB

Series design by FLOK Design, Berlin, Germany
Cover design by Tom Etherington
Creative Advisor: Dennis PAPHITIS

Typeset by CB Editions, London
Printed and bound by Imak Ofset, Istanbul, Turkey

Introduction copyright © 2024 by Gyles Brandreth

Linking text and Illustrations copyright © 1979 by Victorama Limited

The right of Gyles Brandreth to be identified as the author of the
introduction to this work has been asserted by him in accordance with
section 77 of the Copyright, Designs & Patents Act 1998.
All rights reserved.

With the exception of Mrs Beeton's 'nightcap recipes', almost everything
in this book was actually written by Lewis Carroll. I have gathered
material together from a wide variety of sources and in order to make it
'hang together' as neatly as possible I have occasionally been bold enough
– fool enough, you may say – to add a few linking words of my own in
the manner of Lewis Carroll. I hope that he – and you – will forgive
my presumption. The illustrations on pages 12 and 47–48 are by Lewis
Carroll. The remaining illustrations are by Phuz. – Edgar Cuthwellis

A CIP record for this book is available from the British Library

ISBN 978-1-912559-59-6

nottinghilleditions.com

Contents

Do but consider what an excellent thing sleep is: it is so inestimable a jewel that, if a tyrant would give his crown for an hour's slumber, it cannot be bought: of so beautiful a shape is it, that though a man lie with an Empress, his heart cannot beat quite till he leaves her embracements to be at rest with the other: yea, so greatly indebted are we to this kinsman of death, that we owe the better tributary, half our life to him: and there is good cause why we should do so: for sleep is the golden chain that ties health and our bodies together. Who complains of want? of wounds? of cares? of great men's oppressions? of captivity? whilst he sleepeth? Beggars in their beds take as much pleasure as kings: can we therefore surfeit of this delicate ambrosia?

Thomas Dekker (c. 1572–1632)

GYLES BRANDRETH

– Introduction –

Lewis Carroll was extraordinary. Writer, teacher, mathematician, clergyman, photographer, puzzler, poet, he was born on 27 January 1832 and died on 14 January 1898. During his sixty-six years, he did something that very few others have achieved in the entire history of humanity: he created an imaginary world and a raft of characters that became instantly famous across the globe. They are famous still, and, I reckon, will be for the rest of time. Lewis Carroll was a brilliant and complicated human being: tall, slim, awkward, amusing, shy, he had a unique way with words yet suffered from a life-long stammer. He was also an insomniac. This little book (conceived and compiled by me in the 1970s though entirely written by him in Victorian times) will show you how ingeniously this extraordinary man dealt with his sleepless nights.

Lewis Carroll has long been a hero of mine. I fell in love with the heroine of *Alice's Adventures in Wonderland* when I was a little boy living in London in the 1950s and was taken to a stage adaptation of *Through the Looking-Glass* starring a young Juliet Mills as Alice. I became fascinated by him in my early twenties when the veteran British entertainer Cyril Fletcher asked me to create a one-man show based on the life and work of Lewis Carroll. That's when I learnt about his insomnia. In the first act of my one-man play, the great man was in his Oxford college rooms talking to himself as he tried (and failed) to get to sleep. In the second act, he was in bed having dreams (and nightmares) peopled by the characters he had created, from the Mad Hatter to the Frumious Bandersnatch. In the 1980s I devised an *Alice in Wonderland* board game that was produced by Spears Games, the manufacturers of Scrabble – a word-building game very like one Lewis Carroll had devised more than a century before.

In 2010, with the composer Susannah Pearse, I wrote a musical play called *The Last Photograph*, which explored both the mystery of why Lewis Carroll (one of the great photographers of his time) suddenly decided to give up taking pictures and the nature of his relationship with the young actress, Isa Bowman, who famously played Alice on stage and, less conspicuously, holidayed with Carroll in Eastbourne when she was in her late teens and he was in his late forties. It's an intriguing story. He was a most intriguing man.

Lewis Carroll wasn't his real name, of course. He was a clergyman's son, born at All Saints' Vicarage in Daresbury in Cheshire in the north of England, and christened Charles Lutwidge Dodgson, the oldest boy and the third oldest of his parents' eleven children. Most of his male forebears were either army officers or Anglican clergymen. His great-grandfather, another Charles Dodgson, had been Bishop of Elphin in Ireland. His paternal grandfather, again a Charles, had been an army captain, killed in action in Ireland in 1803, when his two sons were still boys. The older of these two, yet another Charles, was Lewis Carroll's father. A brilliant mathematician (he got a double first at Christ Church College, Oxford), he decided against an academic career, married his first cousin, Frances Jane Lutwidge, in 1830, and became a country parson.

When our Charles Dodgson – the Lewis Carroll to be – was eleven, his father was offered the living of Croft-on-Tees and the family moved to Yorkshire where they stayed for the next twenty-five years. Dodgson Senior became the Archdeacon of Richmond and young Charles was sent to Richmond Grammar School, aged twelve, and then to Rugby School, aged fourteen. He was not happy at Rugby. 'I cannot say,' he later wrote, 'that any earthly considerations would induce me to go through my three years again . . . I can honestly say that if I could have been . . . secure from annoyance at night, the hardships of the daily life would have been comparative trifles to bear.' He was not bullied himself, but the younger boys were. According to his first biographer, his nephew, Stuart Dodgson Collingwood, 'even though it is hard for those who have only known him as the gentle and retiring don to believe it, it is nevertheless true that long after he left school, his name was remembered as that of a boy who knew well how to use his fists in defence of a righteous cause.'

He stood up for the younger boys – and he was clever. 'I have not had a more promising boy at his age since I came to Rugby,' reported his mathematics master, R. B. Mayor. He left Rugby at the end of 1849 and went to Christ Church College, Oxford, where he stayed for the rest of his life.

At Oxford, like his father, Charles Dodgson secured a double-first. In 1855 he won the Christ Church Mathematical Lectureship and he later became a Student (or Fellow) of the college. In 1861 he was ordained a deacon in the Church of England, though he was always more a teacher than a preacher. In *The Life and Letters of Lewis Carroll*, Stuart Collingwood wrote, 'his Diary is full of such modest depreciations of himself and his work, interspersed with earnest prayers (too sacred and private to be reproduced here) that God would forgive him the past, and help him to perform His holy will in the future.'

The Reverend Charles Dodgson was clearly a bit of an oddity. He had a slightly ungainly gait because of a knee injury and as a boy he had had a fever that left him hard of hearing in one ear. At seventeen he had severe whooping cough which left him with a chronically weak chest. His stammer – which he called his 'hesitation' – was a nuisance, but not wholly debilitating. He was ready to take part in parlour entertainments, playing charades, singing songs, reciting verse.

He was shy, but not reclusive. He had friends in Oxford and beyond. In 1857 he became friendly with the great John Ruskin. In the early 1860s, he got to know Dante Gabriel Rosetti and his family and took photographs of them in the garden of their house in Chelsea in London. He knew other artists of note, including William Holman Hunt, John Everett Millais and Arthur Hughes. He was a bit of an artist himself. He was a pioneering portrait photographer. And, of course, he was a writer – an inveterate correspondent (he wrote and received as many as 98,721 letters during his lifetime, according to the special letter register which he devised) and a prolific author of verse, fantasy fiction, and scholarly papers.

From a young age, Charles Dodgson was writing poetry and short stories for the Dodgson family's own home-made magazine, *Mischmasch*. At Oxford he began sending humorous contributions to professional publications. In 1855, when he was twenty-three, he admitted, 'I do not think I have yet written anything worthy of real publication (in which I do not include the *Whitby Gazette* or the *Oxonian Advertiser*), but I do not despair of doing so someday.'

In March 1856, he published his first piece of work under the name by which we know him now. The work was a romantic poem entitled 'Solitude' and it appeared in *The Train* under the authorship of 'Lewis Carroll'. The pen name was a play on his real name. 'Lewis' was the anglicised form of Ludovicus, which was the Latin for 'Lutwidge', and 'Carroll' was a popular Irish surname similar to the Latin name Carolus, from which comes the English name 'Charles'. This was Dodgson's thinking: 'Charles Lutwidge' translated into Latin as Carolus Ludovicus, then translated back into English as 'Carroll Lewis', then reversed to make 'Lewis Carroll'. The name was chosen by *The Train*'s editor, Edmund Yates, from a list of four submitted by Dodgson, the others being Louis Carroll, Edgar U. C. Westhill, and Edgar Cuthwellis – the name I have given to the editor of the small volume you are kindly holding in your hand now.

1856 was a notable year in the life of Charles Dodgson. It was the year in which he took up the new art form of photography. It was the year in which 'Lewis Carroll' was born. It was the year, too, when Henry Liddell, formerly headmaster of Westminster School in London, arrived at Christ Church, Oxford, as the new Dean, bringing with him his young family. Charles Dodgson became friends with Liddell's wife, Lorina, and their children, particularly the three Liddell sisters: Lorina (known as Ina), Edith, and Alice. With an adult friend, he would take the Liddell children on rowing trips (first the son, Harry, and later the three girls) along the river Isis.

In the summer of 2023, I was honoured to unveil a plaque on the Isis riverbank marking the anniversary of a rowing trip that proved a landmark in the story of children's literature. On this expedition, on

4 July 1862, with his friend, the Reverend Robinson Duckworth, assisting with the rowing, Dodgson extemporised the outline of the story that would become one of the most famous children's stories ever written. Dodgson invented the tale for Alice Liddell and her sisters and, eventually, at Alice's insistence, he wrote it down. In November 1864, when he was thirty-two and Alice was twelve, he presented her with a handwritten, illustrated manuscript entitled *Alice's Adventures Under Ground*.

In 1863, he had taken the unfinished manuscript to the publisher, Macmillan, who liked it immediately. After alternative titles were rejected – *Alice Among the Fairies*, *Alice's Golden Hour* – the book was published in 1865, with new illustrations by John Tenniel, as *Alice's Adventures in Wonderland*.

The book made Lewis Carroll rich and famous. He was overwhelmed with admiring correspondence from across world. The story went around that Queen Victoria herself was so enamoured of *Alice's Adventures* that she commanded that the author dedicate his next book to her, and was accordingly presented with his next work, a scholarly mathematical volume entitled *An Elementary Treatise on Determinants*. Much embarrassed, Dodgson fiercely denied the story, protesting: 'It is utterly false in every particular: nothing even resembling it has occurred.'

In 1871, he published a sequel, *Through the Looking-Glass and What Alice Found There*. If it is more sombre in tone than the original *Alice*, Lewis Carroll's biographers suggest that may reflect the melancholy that dogged the author for several years following the death of his father in 1868. Even so, the second book was a second commercial triumph, and his next, *The Hunting of the Snark*, published in 1876, did wonderfully well, too. It was something different: a fantastical nonsense poem, illustrated by Henry Holiday, that recounted the adventures of a curious crew of nine tradesmen and one beaver, who set off to find the Snark.

As the years went by there was more, including, in 1889, a two-volume tale of fairy siblings, *Sylvie and Bruno*, in which Lewis Carroll combined two plots set in two worlds: one, rural England; the other, the fairy-tale kingdoms of Elfland, Outland, and elsewhere.

Lewis Carroll was acclaimed as an author and a photographer – but there were some who had doubts about him as a man. A life-long bachelor, he talked openly of his 'child friends' and acknowledged that almost all of them were young girls. 'I am not omnivorous,' he said. He did not much like little boys. And he took far more photographs of young girls than he did of young boys – and in some of those photographs the girls were scantily clad, if dressed at all.

In fairness to Lewis Carroll, painting and photographing children was not so unusual in Victorian times and a careful study (by Roger Taylor and Edward Wakeling) of every surviving photographic print of

Dodgson's (reckoned to be about forty per cent of his output), shows that while just over half of his surviving work depicts young girls, he also made many studies of boys, men, women and landscapes. The variety of his photographic subjects included dolls, dogs, statues, skeletons and trees. His pictures of children were taken with a parent in attendance and many are set in the Liddell garden because natural sunlight was required for good exposures.

He photographed children. He made friends with children. He wrote for children. He made special friends of a number of young girls over a number of years, corresponding amusingly with them, writing and devising poems and puzzles for them and dedicating works to them. In 1893, his sister, Mary, wrote to him about the gossip that was attached to these relationships. On 21 September 1893, he replied to his sister: 'You need not be shocked at my being spoken against. Anybody who is spoken about at all, is sure to be spoken against by somebody: and any action, however innocent in itself, is liable, and not at all unlikely, to be blamed by somebody. If you limit your actions in life to things that nobody can possibly find fault with, you will not do much!' Lewis Carroll told his sister that as a result of his experience he was convinced 'that the opinion of "people" in general is absolutely worthless as a test of right and wrong.' He said that, for him, there were only two tests when 'having some particular girl-friend as a guest': did he have her family's 'full approval for what I do'? And did he 'feel it to be entirely innocent and right in the sight of God'? Lewis Carroll told his sister his conscience was clear.

So it was not a troubled conscience that kept him awake at night. I reckon it was a teeming brain and a wonderfully vivid imagination. He certainly did his best to put his 'wakeful hours' to good use. As you will discover in the pages that follow, he used his inventive genius in all sorts of fantastic ways to keep his mind (and now yours) occupied when sleep eluded him. He even invented a writing tablet that he called 'the nyctograph' that made possible note-taking in the dark.

Fame and fortune did not change him much. He left Oxford during the vacations to go to London (he attended one of the first performances of *Alice in Wonderland* on stage at the Prince of Wales on 30 December 1886); he visited his sister in Guildford; he holidayed in Eastbourne with Isa Bowman. He travelled far and wide in his imagination, of course, but only left the British Isles once, when he went on an expedition to Russia in 1867 in the company of a clergyman friend, the scriptural scholar, Henry Liddon.

Lewis Carroll died of pneumonia, following a bout of influenza, on 14 January 1898, at his sister's home, 'The Chestnuts', in Guildford. It was just four days before the death of Henry Liddell and two weeks before Dodgson would have turned sixty-six. His funeral was held at St Mary's Church and his body is buried at the Mount Cemetery in Guildford. He is commemorated at All Saints' Church in Daresbury with stained-glass windows depicting characters from *Alice's Adventures in Wonderland* and in Poets' Corner in Westminster Abbey with a memorial stone positioned between those of Henry James and D. H. Lawrence.

I hope you will explore more of the work Lewis Carroll. If you can find it on eBay, I hope you will play my *Alice in Wonderland* board game sometime. When it is next revived, I hope you will come to see the musical play that Susannah Pearse and I wrote about him. Meanwhile, if you should chance to have a sleepless night, you have the remedy in your hands: *Lewis Carroll's Guide for Insomniacs* – compiled by me, edited by Edgar Cuthwellis, illustrated by Phuz, but entirely the work of the genius who was Lewis Carroll. Enjoy.

And when eventually you do, sleep tight.

– Pillow Problems –

Calming Calculations

In preparing the second edition of my book *Pillow-Problems Thought Out During Sleepless Nights*, I replaced the words 'sleepless nights' by 'wakeful hours'. The change was made in order to allay the anxiety of kind friends, who had written to me to express their sympathy in my broken-down state of health, believing that I am a sufferer from chronic 'insomnia', and that it is as a remedy for that exhausting malady that I have recommended mathematical calculation.

The original title was not, I fear, wisely chosen; and it certainly *was* liable to suggest a meaning I did not intend to convey, viz. that my 'nights' are very often *wholly* 'sleepless'. This is by no means the case: I have never suffered from 'insomnia': and the over-wakeful hours, that I have had to spend at night, have often been simply the result of the over-sleepy hours I have spent during the preceding evening! Nor is it as a remedy for *wakefulness* that I have suggested mathematical calculation; but as a remedy for the *harassing thoughts* that are apt to invade a wholly-unoccupied mind.

To state the matter logically, the dilemma which

my friends *suppose* me to be in has, for its two horns, the endurance of a sleepless night, and the adoption of some recipe for inducing sleep. Now, so far as *my* experience goes, no such recipe has any effect, unless when you are sleepy, and mathematical calculations would be more likely to delay, than to hasten, the advent of sleep.

The *real* dilemma, which I have had to face, is this: given that the brain is in so wakeful a condition that do what I will, I am *certain* to remain awake for the next hour or so, I must choose between two courses, viz. either to submit to the fruitless self-torture of going through some worrying topic, over and over again, or else to dictate to myself some topic sufficiently absorbing to keep the worry at bay. A mathematical problem *is*, for me, such a topic; and is a benefit, even if it lengthens the wakeful period a little. I believe that an hour of calculation is much better for me than half-an-hour of worry.

Even when it is a matter of the most elementary calculation, the process of arriving at a solution may involve a diverting dialogue, viz. the problem of 'The Two Clocks':

Which is better, a clock that is right only once a year, or a clock that is right twice every day?

'The latter,' you reply, 'unquestionably.' Very good, now attend.

I have two clocks: one doesn't go *at all*, and the

other loses a minute a day: which would you prefer? 'The losing one,' you answer, 'without a doubt.' Now observe: the one which loses a minute a day has to lose twelve hours, or seven hundred and twenty minutes before it is right again, consequently it is only right once in two years, whereas the other is evidently right as often as the time it points to comes round, which happens twice a day. You see that the clock is right *at* eight o'clock? Consequently, when eight o'clock comes round your clock is right.

'Yes, I see *that*,' you reply.

Very good, then you've contradicted yourself *twice*: now get out of the difficulty as best you can, and don't contradict yourself again if you can help it.

You *might* go on to ask, 'How am I to know when eight o'clock *does* come? My clock will not tell me.' Be patient: you know that when eight o'clock comes your clock is right, very good; then your rule is this: keep your eye fixed on your clock, and *the very moment it is right* it will be eight o'clock. 'But—,' you say. There, that'll do; the more you argue the farther you get from the point, so it will be as well to stop.

Here are ten calculations for you to attempt while lying awake at night. The first three are problems, the remainder mere puzzles. The solutions will be found at the back of the book.

1 THE PIGS
   Place twenty-four pigs in four sties so that, as you go round and round, you may always find the number in each sty nearer to ten than the number in the last.

2 THE CHELSEA PENSIONERS
   If 70 per cent have lost an eye, 75 per cent an ear, 80 per cent an arm, 85 per cent a leg: what percentage, *at least*, must have lost all four?

3 THE TWO OMNIBUSES
   Omnibuses start from a certain point, both ways, every 15 minutes. A traveller, starting on foot along with one of them, meets one in 12½ minutes: when will he be overtaken by one?

4 Dreaming of apples on a wall,
     And dreaming often, dear,
   I dreamed that, if I counted all,
     —How many would appear?

5 A stick I found that weighed two pound:
     I sawed it up one day
  In pieces eight of equal weight!
     How much did each piece weigh?
(Everybody says 'a quarter of a pound', which
is wrong.)

6 John gave his brother James a box:
  About it there were many locks.

  James woke and said it gave him pain;
  So gave it back to John again.

  The box was not with lid supplied,
  Yet caused two lids to open wide:

  And all these locks had never a key—
  What kind of a box, then, could it be?

7 What is most like a bee in May?
     'Well, let me think: perhaps—' you say.
  Bravo! You're guessing well today!

8 Three sisters at breakfast
     were feeding the cat,
  The first gave it sole
     —Puss was grateful for that:
  The next gave it salmon
     —which Puss thought a treat:
  The third gave it herring

—which Puss wouldn't eat.
(*Explain the conduct of the cat.*)

9 Said the Moon to the Sun,
    'Is the daylight begun?'
Said the Sun to the Moon,
    'Not a minute too soon.'

'You're a Full Moon,' said he.
    She replied with a frown,
'Well! I never *did* see
    So uncivil a clown!'
(*Query: Why was the moon so angry?*)

10 When the King found that his money was
nearly all gone, and that he really *must* live
more economically, he decided on sending
away most of his Wise Men. There were
some hundreds of them – very fine old men,
and magnificently dressed in green velvet
gowns with gold buttons: if they *had* a fault,
it was that they always contradicted one another when he asked for their advice – and
they certainly ate and drank enormously.
So, on the whole, he was rather glad to get
rid of them. But there was an old law, which
he did not dare to disobey, which said that
there must always be

'Seven blind of both eyes:
    Two blind of one eye:
Four that see with both eyes:
    Nine that see with one eye.'
(*Query: How many did he keep?*)

Magic Numbers

While lying awake in bed consider the curious proper-
ties of certain 'magic numbers':

What is remarkable about 12345679 is that you
can multiply it by 9, or *any* of the first nine multiples of
9, and you will get an answer which simply consists of
a repetition of the same digit. Furthermore, the digit
will be the same as the number of 9s in the multiplier.

$$12345679 \times 9 = 111111111$$
$$12345679 \times 18 = 222222222$$
$$12345679 \times 27 = 333333333$$
$$12345679 \times 36 = 444444444$$
$$12345679 \times 45 = 555555555$$
$$12345679 \times 54 = 666666666$$
$$12345679 \times 63 = 777777777$$
$$12345679 \times 72 = 888888888$$
$$12345679 \times 81 = 999999999$$

Multiply 100001 by any five-digit number you like and you will get a ten-digit answer made up of the five digits repeated twice.

$$100001 \times 12345 = 1234512345$$
$$100001 \times 54321 = 5432154321$$
$$100001 \times 67890 = 6789067890$$
$$100001 \times 98765 = 9876598765$$
$$100001 \times 13579 = 1357913579$$
$$100001 \times 24680 = 2468024680$$
$$100001 \times 99999 = 9999999999$$
$$100001 \times 69696 = 6969669696$$
$$100001 \times 10001 = 1000110001$$

142857 is a most magical 'magic number':

$$142857 \times 2 = 285714$$
$$142857 \times 3 = 428751$$
$$142857 \times 4 = 571428$$
$$142857 \times 5 = 714285$$
$$142857 \times 6 = 857142$$

You will notice that in each case the answer to the sum consists of the same six digits as in the original number and, though starting with a different digit each time, they are in the same order.

What happens when you multiply it by 7?

$$142857 \times 7 = 999999$$

999999 is *not* the answer you expected, but having arrived at it, look where it takes you:

142857 multiplied by 7 equals 999999
 and 999999 divided by 9 equals 111111!

285714 multiplied by 7 equals 1999998
 and 1999998 divided by 9 equals 222222!

428571 multiplied by 7 equals 2999997
 and 2999997 divided by 9 equals 333333!

571428 multiplied by 7 equals 3999996
 and 3999996 divided by 9 equals 444444!

714285 multiplied by 7 equals 4999995
 and 4999995 divided by 9 equals 555555!

857142 multiplied by 7 equals 5999995
 and 5999995 divided by 9 equals 666666!

Tangrams

Tangram is the name given to a Chinese geometrical puzzle consisting of a square dissected into five triangles, a square, and a rhomboid, which can be combined so as to make an infinite variety of figures. Having constructed your own set of Tangrams, attempt to recreate the four following figures. The solutions will be found at the back of the book.

The March Hare

The Cheshire Cat

The Mad Hatter

The Queen of Hearts

The Labyrinth

Make your way from the inside of the labyrinth to the outside – or *vice versa*. You will find the correct path given at the back of the book.

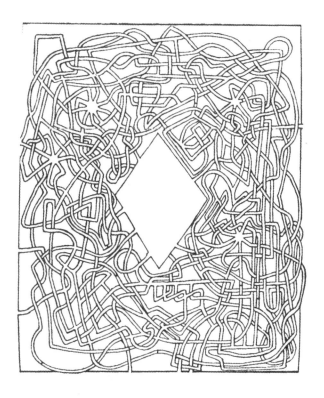

Word Ways

1 A Russian had three sons. The first was named Rab and became a lawyer. The second was named Ymra and became a soldier. The third son became a sailor. What was his name?

2 Find a bird with the letters 'gp' as its nucleus.

3 Find a fruit with the letters 'emo' as its nucleus.

4 'Flit on, cheering angel.' Who is she?

5 'Wild agitator, means well.' Who is he?

The solutions can be found at the back of the book.

Doublets

Just a year ago last Christmas, two young ladies – smarting under that secret scourge of feminine humanity, the having 'nothing to do' – besought me to send them 'some riddles'. But riddles I had none at hand, and therefore set myself to devise some other form of verbal torture which should serve the same purpose. The result of my meditations was a new kind of Puzzle – new at least to me – which, now that it has been fairly tested by a year's experience and commended by many friends, I offer to you.

The rules of the Puzzle are simple enough. Two words are proposed, of the same length; and the puzzle consists in linking these together by interposing other words, each of which shall differ from the next word *in one letter only.* That is to say, one letter may be changed in one of the given words, then one letter in the word so obtained, and so on, till we arrive at the other given word. The letters must not be interchanged among themselves, but each must keep to his own place. As an example, the word 'head' may be changed into 'tail' by interposing the words 'heal, teal, tell, tall'. I call the two given words 'a Doublet', the interposed words 'links', and the entire series 'a Chain', of which I here append an example —

HEAD
h e a l
t e a l
t e l l
t a l l
TAIL

It is, perhaps, needless to state that it is *de rigueur* that the links should be English words, such as might be used in good society.

Links needed

1	Make EEL into PIE	3
2	Turn POOR into RICH	5
3	Prove RAVEN to be MISER	3
4	Change OAT to RYE	3
5	Get WOOD from TREE	7
6	Prove GRASS to be GREEN	7
7	Evolve MAN from APE	5
8	Change CAIN into ABEL	8
9	Make FLOUR into BREAD	5
10	Make TEA HOT	3
11	Run COMB into HAIR	6
12	Prove a ROGUE to be a BEAST	10
13	Change ELM into OAK	7
14	Combine ARMY and NAVY	7
15	Place BEANS on SHELF	7
16	HOOK FISH	6
17	QUELL a BRAVO	10

18	Stow FURIES in BARREL	5
19	BUY an ASS	7
20	Get COAL from MINE	5
21	Pay COSTS in PENCE	9
22	Raise ONE to TWO	7
23	Change BLUE to PINK	8
24	Change BLACK to WHITE	6
25	Change FISH to BIRD	4

The solutions can be found at the back of the book.

Board Game for One

Throw a dice and advance the number of squares indicated. In the event of landing on a square featuring a drawing of any kind, return to the very first square and begin again. Sleep is almost certain to have overwhelmed the player before he reaches the final square.

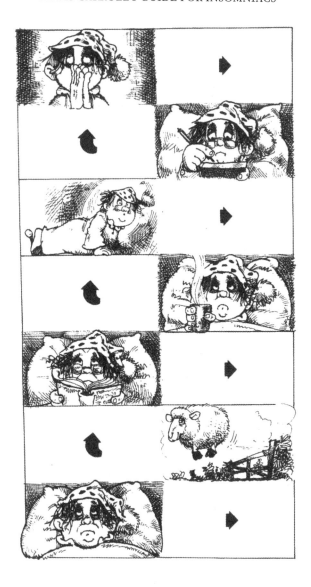

19

– Night Writing –

The Nyctograph

How best to keep warm in bed has long been a dilemma to me. How to write in bed has been a problem too, but it is one I have solved with a simple mechanical appliance that I have named the 'Nyctograph'. I invented it on September 24th 1891, but I do not intend to patent it. Anyone who chooses is welcome to make and sell the article.

Anyone who has tried, as I have often done, the process of getting out of bed at 2 a.m. in a winter night, lighting a candle, and recording some happy thought which would probably be otherwise forgotten, will agree with me it entails much discomfort. All I have now to do, if I wake and think of something I wish to record, is to draw from under the pillow a small memorandum book, containing my Nyctograph, write a few lines, or even a few pages, without even putting the hands outside the bed-clothes, replace the book, and go to sleep again.

There is an ingenious machine already made and sold (I bought mine from Messrs Elliot, 101 St Martin's Lane), where you write a line of MS inside a narrow oblong opening, then turn a handle till you hear a click; this shifts the paper upwards and gives a fresh surface for another line of MS.

I tried to put this into a more portable shape, by cutting a series of oblong apertures in a piece of pasteboard the size of a page of a small memorandum book; but the writing is apt to be illegible, as it is difficult to know where you are, and you constantly come against the edge of the aperture when you wish to go further in order to make the loop of an 'h' or the tail of a 'y'. Then I tried rows of square holes, each to hold one letter (quarter of an inch square I found a very convenient size), and this proved a much better plan than the former; but the letters were still apt to be illegible. Then I said to myself 'Why not invent a square alphabet, using only dots at the corners, and lines along the sides?' I soon found that, to make the writing easy to read, it was necessary to know where each square began. This I secured by the rule that *every* square-letter should contain a large black dot in the North West corner. Also I found that it would cause confusion to have any symbol which used only the West side of the square. These limitations reduced the number of available symbols to 31, of which I selected 26 for the letters of the alphabet, and succeeded in getting 23 of them to have a distinct resemblance to the letters they were to represent.

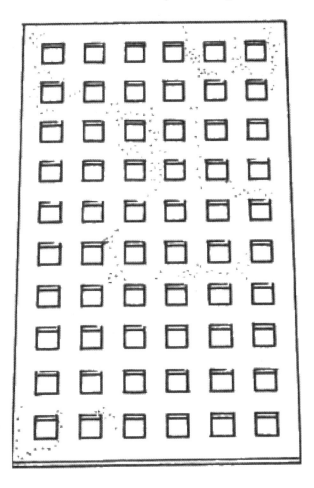

In the following list, I call the North East corner '2', the South West corner '3', and the South East corner '4'. Also I have bracketed letters whose symbols run in pairs, each being the reverse of the other. Every symbol is assumed to have a large dot in its North West corner.

		Corners	Sides
	A	4	none
	B	2, 4	W
{	C	none	N,W,S
	D	none	N,E,S
	E	none	N
{	F	4	N,W
	G	2	W,S
	H	none	W,E
	I	none	S
	J	none	E,S
	K	4	W
	L	none	W,S
{	M	none	N,W,E
	N	none	W,E,S
	O	none	N,W,E,S
{	P	2	W
	Q	none	E
	R	3	N,E
{	S	none	N,W
	T	none	N,E
	U	2	none
	V	2, 4	none
	W	2	S
{	X	3	N
	Y	4	N
	Z	none	N,S

Resemblance to letters, etc.
right-hand side of 'A'
vertical line of 'B', with dots to stand for the semi-circles.
obvious
obvious; also reverse of preceding symbol
top of 'E'; taken as simplest symbol for commonest letter
obvious; dot stands for cross-piece which has fallen off
analogous to symbol for 'C'; also reverse of preceding symbol
obvious
like 'i', vertical line having fallen down
like 'j', dot having slipped to one side
vertical line, and foot, of 'K'
obvious
like 'm', with central vertical erased
reverse of preceding symbol
obvious
vertical line of 'p', with dot to stand for the semicircle
vertical line of 'q', with dot to stand for the semicircle;
   also reverse of preceding symbol
lower part of 'R'
like old-fashioned 's'
left-hand part of 'T'; also reverse of preceding symbol
tops of 'U'
corners of 'V'
like 2 'V' symbols, with lower corners connected by a line
no likeness claimed
ditto, but is reverse of preceding symbol
upper and lower lines of 'Z'

	Corners	Sides
'figures'	2, 3	none
'date'	2, 3, 4	none
'letters'	3, 4	none
'and'	3	E
'the'	3, 4	N

When the symbols are to represent figures, they should be the symbols for 10 of the letters, as follows:

	Letters	Reasons for Selection
1	B	first consonant
2	D	initial of 'duo' and 'deux'
3	T	initial of 'three'
4	F	initial of 'four'
5	L	means '50'
6	S	initial of 'six'
7	M	finial of 'septem'
8	H	initial of 'huit'; also resembles '8'
9	N	initial of 'nine'
0	Z	initial of 'zero'

These 10 letters are a portion of my 'Memoria Technica', in which (by assigning 2 consonants to each digit, and assigning no meanings to vowels and 'Y') I can always represent any date, or other number, by a *real*

Meaning

corners of 'F'; means 'symbols will now represent figures'

corners of a square 'D'; means 'next 6 symbols will represent date, 2 standing for day of month, 2 for month, and 2 for year of century (e.g. '070305' would represent 7th March 1805)

corners of 'L'; means 'symbols will now represent letters again'

symbol for 'A' put upright; and right-hand portions of symbols for 'N' and 'D'

upper portion of symbol for 'T'; feet of symbol for 'H'; and symbol for 'E'

---

word: the other 10 consonants being as follows: '1, c; 2, w; 3, j; 4, q; 5, v; 6, x; 7, p; 8, k; 9, g; 0, r.' There are reasons for selection in all these pairs, except '3, j', which had to pair off as the sole survivors.

Rules for Letter Writing

Much of my correspondence is conducted late at night. Indeed it is not uncommon for me still to be writing letters at three o'clock in the morning. Whatever time *you* choose to conduct *your* correspondence, the art of letter-writing involves certain rules that should *never* be broken be it ever so late – or so early.

HOW TO BEGIN A LETTER

If the Letter is to be in answer to another, begin by getting out that other letter and reading it through, in order to refresh your memory, as to what it is you have to answer, and as to your correspondent's *present address* (otherwise you will be sending your letter to his regular address in *London*, though he has been careful in writing to give you his *Torquay* address in full).

Next, Address and Stamp the Envelope. 'What! Before writing the *Letter*?' Most certainly. And I'll tell you what will happen if you don't. You will go on writing till the last moment, and, just in the middle of the last sentence, you will become aware that 'time's up!' Then comes the hurried wind-up – the wildly-scrawled signature – the hastily-fastened envelope, which comes open in the post – the address, a mere hieroglyphic – the horrible discovery that you've forgotten to replenish your Stamp-case – the frantic appeal, to everyone in the house, to lend you a stamp – the headlong rush to the Post Office, arriving, hot and gasping, just after the box has closed – and finally, a week afterwards, the return of the Letter, from the Dead-Letter Office, marked 'address illegible'!

Next, put your own address, *in full*, at the top of the note-sheet. It is an aggravating thing—I speak from bitter experience—when a friend, staying at some new address, heads his letter 'Dover', simply, assuming that you can get the rest of the address from his previous letter, which perhaps you have destroyed.

Next, put the date *in full*. It is another aggravating thing, when you wish, years afterwards, to arrange a series of letters, to find them dated 'Feb. 17', 'Aug. 2', without any *year* to guide you as to which comes first. And never, never, dear Madam (N.B. this remark is addressed to ladies *only*: no *man* would ever do such a thing), put 'Wednesday', simply, as the date!

'That way madness lies.'

HOW TO GO ON WITH A LETTER

Here is a golden Rule to begin with. *Write legibly.* The average temper of the human race would be perceptibly sweetened, if everybody obeyed this Rule! A great deal of the bad writing in the world comes simply from writing *too quickly*. Of course you reply, 'I do it to save *time*.' A very good object, no doubt: but what right have you to do it at your friend's expense? Isn't *his* time as valuable as yours? Years ago, I used to receive letters from a friend – and very interesting letters too – written in one of the most atrocious hands ever invented. It generally took me about a *week* to read one of his letters. I used to carry it about in my pocket, and take it out at leisure times, to puzzle over the riddles which composed it – holding it in different positions and at different distances, till at last the meaning of some hopeless scrawl would flash upon me, when I at once wrote down the English under it; and, when several had been thus guessed, the context would help with the others, till at last the whole series of hieroglyphics was deciphered. If *all* one's friends wrote like that, Life would be entirely spent in reading their letters!

My second Rule is, don't fill *more* than a page and a half with apologies for not having written sooner!

The best subject, to *begin* with, is your friend's last letter. Write with the letter open before you. Answer his questions, and make any remarks his letter suggests. *Then* go on to what you want to say yourself. This arrangement is more courteous, and pleasanter for the reader, than to fill the letter with your own invaluable remarks, and then hastily answer your friend's questions in a postscript. Your friend is much more likely to enjoy your wit, *after* his own anxiety for information has been satisfied.

A few more Rules may fitly be given here, for correspondence that has unfortunately become *controversial*.

One is, *don't repeat yourself.* When once you have said your say, fully and clearly, on a certain point, and have failed to convince your friend, *drop that subject*: to repeat your arguments, all over again, will simply lead to his doing the same.

Another Rule is, when you have written a letter that you feel may possibly irritate your friend, however necessary you may have felt it to so express yourself, *put it aside till the next day.* Then read it over again, and fancy it addressed to yourself. This will often lead to your writing it all over again, taking out a lot of the vinegar and pepper, and putting in honey instead, and thus making a *much* more palatable dish of it! If, when you have done your best to write inoffensively, you still feel that it will probably lead to further controversy, *keep a copy of it.* There is very little use, months afterwards, in pleading 'I am almost sure I never expressed myself as you say: to the best of my recollection I said so-and-so'. *Far* better to be able to write: 'I did *not* express myself so: these are the words I used.'

My fifth Rule is, if your friend makes a severe remark, either leave it unnoticed, or make your reply distinctly *less* severe: and if he makes a friendly remark, tending towards 'making-up' the little difference that has arisen between you, let your reply be distinctly *more* friendly. If, in picking a quarrel, each party declined to go more than three-eighths of the way, and if, in making friends, each was ready to go five-eighths of the way – why, there would be more reconciliations than quarrels! Which is like the Irishman's remonstrance to his gad-about daughter—'Shure, you're *always* goin' out! You go out *three* times, for *wanst* that you come in!'

My sixth Rule (and my last remark about controversial correspondence) is, *don't try to have the last word!* How many a controversy would be nipped in the bud, if each was anxious to let the *other* have the last word! Never mind how telling a rejoinder you leave unuttered: never mind your friend's supposing that you are silent from lack of anything to say: let the thing drop, as soon as it is possible without discourtesy: remember 'speech is silvern, but silence is golden'! (N.B.—If you are a gentleman, and your friend is a lady, this Rule is superfluous: *you won't get the last word!*)

My seventh Rule is, if it should ever occur to you to write, jestingly, in *dispraise* of your friend, be sure you exaggerate enough to make the jesting *obvious*: a word spoken in *jest*, but taken as earnest, may lead to very serious consequences.

My eighth Rule. When you say, in your letter, 'I enclose cheque for £5,' or 'I enclose John's letter for you to see,' leave off writing for a moment – go and get the document referred to – and *put it into the envelope.* Otherwise, you are pretty certain to find it lying about, after the post has gone!

My ninth Rule. When you get to the end of a notesheet, and find you have more to say, take another piece of paper – a whole sheet, or a scrap, as the case may demand: but whatever you do, *don't cross!* Remember the old proverb '*Cross-writing makes cross reading*'. 'The *old* proverb?' you say, inquiringly, '*How* old?' Well, not so *very* ancient, I must confess. In fact, I'm afraid I invented it while writing this paragraph! Still, you know, 'old' is a *comparative* term. I think you would be *quite* justified in addressing a chicken, just out of the shell, as 'Old boy!' *when compared* with another chicken, that was only half-out!

HOW TO END A LETTER

If doubtful whether to end with 'yours faithfully', or 'yours truly', or 'yours most truly', &c. (there are at least a dozen varieties, before you reach 'yours affectionately'), refer to your correspondent's last letter, and make your winding-up *at least as friendly as his*: in fact, even if a shade *more* friendly, it will do no harm!

A Postscript is a very useful invention: but it is *not* meant (as so many ladies suppose) to contain the real *gist* of the letter: it serves rather to throw into the shade any little matter we do *not* wish to make a fuss about. For example, you friend had promised to execute a commission for you in town, but forgot it, thereby putting you to great inconvenience: and he now writes to apologise for his negligence. It would be cruel, and needlessly crushing, to make it the main subject of your reply. How much more gracefully it comes in thus: 'P.S. Don't distress yourself any more about having omitted that little matter in town. I won't deny that it *did* put my plans out a little, at the time, but it's all right now. I often forget things myself: and "those who live in glasshouses mustn't throw stones", you know!'

When you take your letters to the Post, *carry them in your hand*. If you put them in your pocket you will take a long country-walk (I speak from experience), passing the Post-Office *twice*, going and returning, and, when you get home, you will find them *still* in your pocket.

Letter to a Child-Friend

Lately I have been awfully busy, and I've had to write *heaps* of letters – wheelbarrows full, almost. And it tires me so that generally I go to bed again the next minute after I get up: and sometimes I go to bed again a minute *before* I get up! Did you ever hear of any one being so tired as *that*? . . .

The letters I enjoy writing most of all are the ones I send to the child-friends who have brightened my life. Usually the child becomes so entirely a different being as she grows into a woman, that our friendship has to change too: and *that* it usually does by gliding down from a loving intimacy into an acquaintance that merely consists of a smile and a bow when we meet!

But while my child-friends remain *children* I can write them as I please, viz:

Christ Church,
Oxford
December 15, 1875.

My dear Magdalen, — I want to explain to you why I did not call yesterday. I was sorry to miss you, but you see I had so many conversations on the way. I tried to explain to the people in the street that I was going to see you, but they wouldn't listen; they said they were in a hurry, which was rude. At last I met a wheel-barrow that I thought would attend to me, but I couldn't make out what was in it. I saw some features at first, then I looked through a tel-escope, and found it was a countenance; then I looked through a microscope, and found it was a face! I thought it was rather like me, so I fetched a large looking-glass to make sure, and then to my great joy I found it was me. We shook hands, and were just beginning to talk, when myself came up and joined us, and we had quite a pleasant conversation. I said, 'Do you remember when we all met at Sandown?' and myself said, 'It was very jolly there; there was a child called Magdalen,' and me said, 'I used to like her a little; not much you know – only a little.' Then it was time for us to go to the train, and who do you think came to the station to see us off? You would never guess, so I must tell you. They were two very dear friends of mine, who happen to be here just now, and beg to be allowed to sign this letter as your affectionate friends,

Lewis Carroll and C. L. Dodgson.

The Alphabet Cipher

In order to write in the dark you may make use of my Nyctograph. In order to keep others 'in the dark' as to what you are writing, you should use the Alphabet Cipher.

Each column of this table forms a dictionary of symbols representing the alphabet: thus, in the A column, the symbol is the same as the letter represented; in the B column, A is represented by B, B by c, and so on.

To use the table, some word or sentence should be agreed on by two correspondents. This may be called the 'key-word', or 'key-sentence', and should be carried in the memory only.

In sending a message, write the key-word over it, letter for letter, repeating it as often as may be necessary: the letters of the key-word will indicate which column is to be used in translating each letter of the message, the symbols for which should be written underneath: then copy out the symbols only, and destroy the first paper. It will now be impossible for anyone, ignorant of the key-word, to decipher the message, even with the help of the table.

For example, let the key-word be *vigilance,* and the message 'meet me on Tuesday evening at seven', the first paper will read as follows —

v i g i l ancevi g i l ancevigi lancevi
m e e t meontue s dayeveni ngatseven
h mkbx ebpxpmyl l yrxii qt oltfgzzv

The second will contain only 'hmkbxebpxpmyl-lyrxiiqtoltfgzzv'.

The receiver of the message can, by the same process, retranslate it into English.

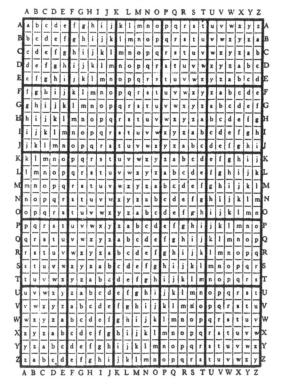

My Fairy

I have a fairy by my side
   Which says I must not sleep,
When once in pain I loudly cried
   It said 'You must not weep'.

If, full of mirth, I smile and grin,
   It says 'You must not laugh',
When once I wished to drink some gin
   It said 'You must not quaff'.

When once a meal I wished to taste
   It said 'You must not bite';
When to the wars I went in haste
   It said 'You must not fight'.

'What may I do?' at length I cried,
   Tired of the painful task.
The fairy quietly replied,
   And said 'You must not ask'.

Moral: 'You mustn't.'

– Rhymes at Midnight –

Again and again I have said to myself, on lying down at night, after a day embittered by some vexatious matter, 'I will *not* think of it any more! I have gone through it all, thoroughly. It can do no good whatever to go through it again. I *will* think of something else!' And in another ten minutes I have found myself, once more, in the very thick of the miserable business, and torturing myself, to no purpose, with all the old troubles.

Now it is not possible – this, I think, all psychologists will admit – by any effort of volition, to carry out the resolution 'I will *not* think of so-and-so.' (Witness the common trick, played on a child, of saying 'I'll give you a penny if you'll stand in that corner for five minutes, and *not once* think of strawberry-jam.' No human child ever yet won the tempting wager!) But it *is* possible – as I am most thankful to know – to carry out the resolution 'I *will* think of so-and-so.' Once fasten the attention upon a subject so chosen, and you will find that the worrying subject, which you desire to banish, is *practically* annulled. It may recur, from time to time – just looking in at the door, so to speak; but it will find itself so coldly received, and will get so little attention paid to it, that it will, after a while, cease to be any worry at all.

Perhaps I may venture, for a moment, to use a more serious tone, and to point out that there are mental troubles, much worse than mere worry, for which an absorbing subject of thought may serve as a remedy. There are sceptical thoughts, which seem for the moment to uproot the firmest faith; there are blasphemous thoughts, which dart unbidden into the most reverent souls; there are unholy thoughts, which torture, with their hateful presence, the fancy that would fain be pure.

Verses with a Moral

Composing original verses in one's head while lying in bed is mental *work* that *relaxes* one. Should the verses have a moral they may even *uplift* one at the same time.

BROTHER AND SISTER

'Sister, sister, go to bed!
Go and rest your weary head.'
Thus the prudent brother said.

'Do you want a battered hide,
Or scratches to your face applied?'
Thus his sister calm replied.

'Sister, do not raise my wrath.
I'd make you into mutton broth
As easily as kill a moth!'

The sister raised her beaming eye
And looked on him indignantly
And sternly answered, 'Only try!'

Off to the cook he quickly ran,
'Dear Cook, please lend a frying-pan
To me as quickly as you can.'

'And wherefore should I lend it you?'
'The reason, Cook, is plain to view.
I wish to make an Irish stew.'

'What meat is in that stew to go?'
'My sister'll be the contents!'
     'Oh!'
'You'll lend the pan to me, Cook?'
     'No!'

Moral: Never stew your sister.

PUNCTUALITY

Man naturally loves delay,
    And to procrastinate:
Business put off from day to day
    Is always done too late.

Let every hour be in its place
    Firm fixed, nor loosely shift,
And well enjoy the vacant space,
    As though a birthday gift.

And when the hour arrives, be *there.*
    Where'er that 'there' may be;
Uncleanly hands or ruffled hair
    Let no one ever see.

If dinner at 'half-past' be placed,
    At 'half-past' then be dressed.
If at a 'quarter-past' make haste
    To be down with the rest.

Better to be before your time,
    Than e'er to be behind;
To ope the door while strikes the chime,
    That shows a punctual mind.

Moral

Let punctuality and care
    Seize every flitting hour,
So shalt thou cull a floweret fair,
    E'en from a fading flower.

Dilutions

Why is it that Poetry has never yet been subjected to that process of Dilution which has proved so advantageous to her sister-art Music? The Diluter gives us first a few notes of some well-known air, then a dozen bars of his own, then a few more notes of the air, and so on alternately; thus saving the listener, if not from all risk of recognising the melody at all, at least from the too-exciting transports which it might produce in a more concentrated form. The process is termed 'setting' by Composers, and any one that has ever experienced the emotion of being unexpectedly set down in a heap of mortar, will recognise the truthfulness of this happy phrase.

For truly, just as the genuine Epicure lingers lovingly over a morsel of supreme Venison – whose every fibre seems to murmur 'Excelsior!' – yet swallows, ere returning to the toothsome dainty, great mouthfuls of oatmeal-porridge and winkles: and just as the perfect Connoisseur in Claret permits him but one delicate sip, and then tosses off a pint or more of boarding-school beer: so also—

> I never loved a dear Gazelle—
> *Nor anything that cost me much:*
> *High prices profit those who sell,*
> *But why should I be fond of such?*

To glad me with his soft black eye
  My son comes trotting home from school;
  He's had a fight but can't tell why—
  He always was a little fool!

But, when he came to know me well,
  He kicked me out, her testy Sire:
  And when I stained my hair, that Belle
  Might note the change, and thus admire

And love me, it was sure to dye
  A muddy green, or staring blue:
  Whilst one might trace, with half an eye,
  The still triumphant carrot through.

The first line of each verse is taken from a quatrain in Thomas Moore's poem *The Fire Worshippers*. I 'diluted' Moore by adding the lines in italic. As a diversion during a sleepless night, choose a favourite verse by one of the great poets and 'dilute' it with some additional lines of your own.

If Dilution is impossible – alas, you can remember *none* of the verses of the great poets! – you will have no alternative but to compose original Acrostics, Charades and Limericks.

Acrostic

This acrostic was composed for a favourite child-friend, Agnes Georgina Hull.

Around my lonely hearth tonight,
    Ghostlike the shadows wander:
Now here, now there, a childish sprite,
Earthborn and yet as angel bright,
    Seems near me as I ponder.

Gaily she shouts: the laughing air
    Echoes her note of gladness—
Or bends herself with earnest care
Round fairy-fortress to prepare
Grim battlement or turret-stair—
    In childhood's merry madness!

New raptures still hath youth in store.
    Age may but fondly cherish
Half-faded memories of yore—
Up, craven heart! repine no more!
Love stretches hands from shore to shore:
    Love is, and shall not perish!

Charade

One may combine a puzzle with a poem and create a versified riddle, like this Charade:

A CHARADE.

[NB FIVE POUNDS will be
given to any one who succeeds in
writing an original poetical Cha-
-rade, introducing the line "My
First is followed by a bird," but
making no use of the answer to
this Charade   Ap 8 1878
        (signed)
            Lewis Carroll]

My First is singular at best
    More plural is my Second
My Third is far the pluralest —
So plural-plural, I protest,
    It scarcely can be reckoned!

My First is followed by a bird
    My Second by believers
In magic and my simple Third
Follows, too often, hopes absurd,
    And plausible deceivers

My First to get at wisdom tries —
    A failure melancholy!
My Second men revere as wise:
My Third from heights of wisdom flies
    To depths of frantic folly!

My First is ageing day by day,
  My Second's age is ended
My Third enjoys an age, they say,
That never seems to fade away,
  Through centuries extended!

My Whole! I need a Poet's pen
  To paint her myriad phases
The monarch, and the slave, of men —
A mountain-summit, and a den
  Of dark and deadly mazes!

A flashing light — a fleeting shade —
  Beginning, end, and middle
Of all that human art hath made,
Or wit devised! Go, seek her aid,
  If you would guess my riddle!

The solution to the Charade can be found at the back of the book.

Limericks

There was a young lady of station,
'I love man' was her sole exclamation:
    But when men cried, 'You flatter,'
    She replied, 'Oh! no matter,
Isle of Man is the true explanation.'

There was an old farmer of Readall,
Who made holes in his face with a needle,
    Then went *far* deeper in
    Than to pierce through the skin,
And yet strange to say he was made beadle.

There was an eccentric old draper,
Who wore a hat made of brown paper,
    It went up to a point,
    Yet it looked out of joint,
The cause of which *he* said was 'vapour'.

There was once a young man of Oporta,
Who daily got shorter and shorter,
    The reason he said
    Was the hod on his head,
Which was filled with the *heaviest* mortar.

His sister, named Lucy O'Finner,
Grew constantly thinner and thinner;
  The reason was plain,
  She slept out in the rain,
And was never allowed any dinner.

– Ghosts and Nightcaps –

Phantasmagoria

One winter night, at half-past nine,
   Cold, tired, and cross, and muddy,
I had come home, too late to dine,
And supper, with cigars and wine,
   Was waiting in the study.

There was a strangeness in the room,
   And Something white and wavy
Was standing near me in the gloom—
I took it for the carpet-broom
   Left by that careless slavey.

But presently the Thing began
   To shiver and to sneeze:
On which I said 'Come, come, my man!
That's a most inconsiderate plan,
   Less noise there, if you please!'

'I've caught a cold,' the Thing replies,
   'Out there upon the landing.'
I turned to look in some surprise,
And there, before my very eyes,
   A Little Ghost was standing!

When encountering a ghost for the first time it is necessary to remain as calm as may be and to retain the normal courtesies of civilised society, viz. on meeting a ghost in the street after dark a gentleman should always raise his hat. However should you be lying in bed affeared lest you might meet a ghost, having never met one before, the simplest method of allaying those fears is to conjure up a shadowy ghost of your own.

Shadow Play

I dreamt I dwelt in marble halls,
And each damp thing that creeps and crawls
Went wobble-wobble on the walls.

By positioning your hands so as to form certain config-
urations and by placing your hands between a source
of light – be it a moonbeam or a lamp – and a blank
wall, you can ensure that what goes wobble-wobble on
your bedroom wall is not a fiend but a friend.

The White Rabbit

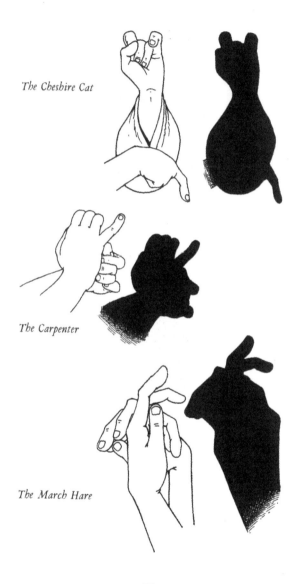

The Cheshire Cat

The Carpenter

The March Hare

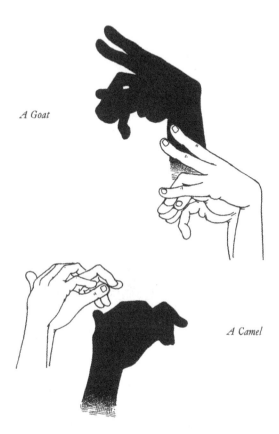

A Goat

A Camel

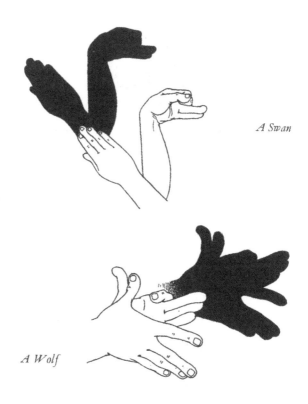

A Swan

A Wolf

Eat Wisely

Methought I walked a dismal place
   Dim horrors all around;
The air was thick with many a face,
   And black as night the ground.

I saw a monster come with speed,
   Its face of grimmliest green,
On human beings used to feed,
   Most dreadful to be seen.

I could not speak, I could not fly,
   I fell down in that place,
I saw the monster's horrid eye
   Come leering in my face!

Amidst my scarcely-stifled groans,
   Amidst my moanings deep,
I heard a voice, 'Wake! Mr Jones,
   You're screaming in your sleep!'

Restless nights and dreams that frighten and alarm us are all too frequently the result of an unfortunate evening meal. In a desultory conversation on a point connected with the dinner at our high table, the Senior Censor incidentally remarked to me that lobster-sauce, 'though a necessary adjunct to turbot, was not entirely wholesome'. It is entirely unwholesome. I never ask for it without reluctance. I never take a second spoonful without a feeling of apprehension on the subject of possible nightmare.

Eat Well

If peace of mind and a restful night are wanted, what one chooses to eat at the dinner table is a matter of considerable moment. How one chooses to *behave* at the dinner table is of no less significance. Indeed, in the hope of being of some assistance to those diners-out who are unacquainted with the usages of society I append a few 'hints for etiquette' that I trust may be of some small value:

In proceeding to the dining-room, the gentleman gives one arm to the lady he escorts – it is unusual to offer both.

The practice of taking soup with the next gentleman but one is now wisely discontinued; but the custom of asking your host his opinion of the weather immediately on the removal of the first course still prevails.

To use a fork with your soup, intimating at the same time to your hostess that you are reserving the spoon for the beefsteaks, is a practice wholly exploded.

On meat being placed before you, there is no possible objection to your eating it, if so disposed; still, in all such delicate cases, be guided entirely by the conduct of those around you.

It is always allowable to ask for artichoke jelly with your boiled venison; however, there are houses where this is not supplied.

The method of helping roast turkey with two carving-forks is practicable, but deficient in grace.

We do not recommend the practice of eating cheese with a knife and fork in one hand, and a spoon and wineglass in the other; there is a kind of awkwardness in the action which no amount of practice can entirely dispel.

As a general rule, do not kick the shins of the opposite gentleman under the table, if personally unacquainted with him; your pleasantry is liable to be misunderstood – a circumstance at all times unpleasant.

Proposing the health of the boy in buttons immediately on the removal of the cloth is a custom springing from regard to his tender years, rather than from a strict adherence to the rules of etiquette.

Nightcaps

How one behaves and what one eats at the dinner-table are matters of consequence. What one drinks at dinner is a matter of importance as well. When they are dining at my table I offer my guests a variety of drinks. My lady-guests mostly prefer draught-lemonade—but they can have any of the following beverages: (1) bottled lemonade; (2) ginger-beer; (3) beer; (4) water; (5) milk; (6) vinegar; (7) ink. Nobody has yet chosen either No. 6 or No. 7 . . .

In the matter of 'nightcaps' I am indebted to Mrs Samuel Beeton for the following suggestions. The first three beverages are *entirely* soothing. The remaining three may be considered more *stimulating.*

COCOA

Ingredients: Allow 2 teaspoonfuls of the prepared cocoa, or one of Cadbury's Cocoa Essence, to 1 breakfast-cup of boiling milk and boiling water.
Mode: Put the cocoa into a breakfast-cup, pour over it sufficient cold milk to make it into a smooth paste; then add equal quantities of boiling milk and boiling water, and stir all well together. Care must be taken not to allow the milk to get burnt, as it will entirely spoil the flavour of the preparation. The rock cocoa, or that bought in a solid piece, should be scraped, and

made in the same manner, taking care to rub down all the lumps before the boiling liquid is added. All cocoa is better boiled for a minute or two.

Sufficient: 2 teaspoonfuls of prepared cocoa, or 1 of Cadbury's Cocoa Essence, for 1 breakfast-cup, or 1/4 oz. of the rock cocoa for the same quantity.

MILK DRINK

Ingredients: 1 pint of new milk, 1 pint of water, salt to taste, 1 egg.

Mode: Pour the milk and water together, beat up the egg with the salt, and add it, mixing thoroughly.

Time: 2 minutes. Average Cost, 3d.

Sufficient to make 1 quart.

BEEF-TEA (*Baron Liebig's Method*)

Mode: Mince very finely 1/2 lb of lean beef, put it in a glass or cup (not in metal) and pour on it 3/4 pint of cold water, 4 drops of muriatic acid, and half a salt-spoonful of salt. Let it stand for an hour, then strain it through a hair sieve, and rinse the residue with another 1/4 pint of water.

This is quite transparent, and contains the albumen in solution. It should be taken cold, or, if heated, it should not be above 120° Fahr.

EGG WINE

Ingredients: 1 egg, 2 tablespoonfuls of cold water, 1 glass of sherry, sugar and grated nutmeg to taste.

Mode: Beat the egg, mixing with it a tablespoonful of cold water; make the wine and the rest of the water hot, but not boiling: pour it on the egg, stirring all the time. Add sufficient lump sugar to sweeten the mixture, and a little grated nutmeg; put all into a very clean saucepan, set it on a gentle fire, and stir the contents one way until they thicken, but *do not allow them to boil.* Serve in a glass with snippets of toasted bread or plain crisp biscuits. When the egg is not warmed, the mixture will be found easier of digestion, but it is not so pleasant a drink.

Sufficient for 1 person.

CLARET CUP

Ingredients: 1 bottle of claret, 1 pint bottle of champagne, 1 bottle of seltzer or soda, 1 glass of maraschino, 2 peaches or a few slices of pineapple, 3 or 4 tablespoonfuls of powdered sugar, borage.

Mode: Put the sugar in a jug and pour over the claret and liqueur, and stand in ice. When wanted, put the peaches sliced, or the pineapple, into a bowl, then pour over the contents of the jug, the champagne and the seltzer, both of which may be iced, put in the borage

and let it stand for a few minutes before serving.
Average Cost, 5s.
Sufficient for 6 persons.

A CAPITAL 'NIGHTCAP'

Ingredients: 4 lumps of sugar, 4 drops of essence of cloves, 1/2 pint of strong ale, 1 wineglassful of brandy.
Mode: Drop the essence on the sugar, put all the ingredients into a saucepan, and drink the mixture hot, just before bedtime.
Average Cost, 6d.

Good Morning

'Heaviness may endure for a night,
but joy cometh in the morning.'

Whatever the horrors of the night, day always comes. Do you not know that delicious dreamy feeling when one first wakes on a summer morning, with the twitter of birds in the air, and the fresh breeze coming in at the open window – when, lying lazily with eyes half shut, one sees as in a dream green boughs waving, or waters rippling in a golden light? It is a pleasure very near to sadness, bringing tears to one's eyes like a beautiful picture or poem. And if you are a child is not that a Mother's sweet voice that summons you to rise? To rise and forget, in the bright sunlight, the ugly dreams that frightened you so when all was dark – to rise and enjoy another happy day, first kneeling to thank that unseen Friend, who sends you the beautiful sun?

A nightcap of a different sort: what the well-dressed clergyman wears to bed.

– Solutions –

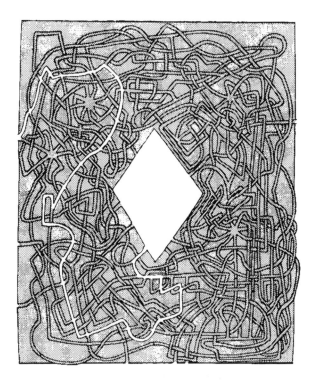

Calming Calculations

1 Place 8 pigs in the first sty, 10 in the second, nothing in the third, and 6 in the fourth: 10 is nearer ten than 8; nothing is nearer ten than 10; 6 is nearer ten than nothing; and 8 is nearer ten than 6.

2 Ten. Adding the wounds together, we get 70 + 75 + 80 + 85 = 310, among 100 men; which gives 3 to each, and 4 to 10 men. Therefore the least percentage is 10.

3 In 6¼ minutes.

4 Ten.

5 In Shylock's bargain for the flesh was found
    No mention of the blood that flowed around:
So when the stick was sawed in eight,
    The sawdust lost diminished from the weight.

6 As curly-headed Jemmy was sleeping in bed,
His brother John gave him a blow on the head;
James opened his eyelids, and spying his brother,
Doubled his fist, and gave him another.
This kind of box then is not so rare;
The lids are the eyelids, the locks are the hair,
And so every schoolboy can tell to his cost,
The key to the tangles is constantly lost.

7 'Twixt 'Perhaps' and 'May be'
    Little difference we see:

Let the question go round,
    The answer is found.

8 That salmon and sole Puss should think very grand
        Is no such remarkable thing.
    For more of these dainties Puss took up her stand;
    But when the third sister stretched out her fair hand
        Pray why should Puss swallow her ring?

9 'In these degenerate days', we oft hear said,
        'Manners are lost and chivalry is dead!'
    No wonder, since in high exalted spheres
        The same degeneracy, in fact, appears.
    The Moon, in social matters interfering,
        Scolded the Sun, when early in appearing:
    And the rude Sun, her gentle sex ignoring,
        Called her a fool, thus her pretensions flooring.

10 Five seeing, and seven blind
        Give us twelve, in all, we find;
    But all of these, 'tis very plain,
        Come into account again.
    For take notice, it may be true,
        That those blind of one eye are blind for two;
    And consider contrariwise,
        That to see with your eye you may have your eyes:
    So setting one against the other—
        For a mathematician no great bother—
    And working the sum, you will understand
        That sixteen wise men still trouble the land.

Word Ways

1 Yvan. Rab is 'bar' reversed. Ymra is 'army' reversed.

2 Magpie.

3 Lemon.

4 The phrase is an anagram of 'Florence Nightingale'.

5 The phrase is an anagram of 'William Ewart Gladstone'.

Tangrams

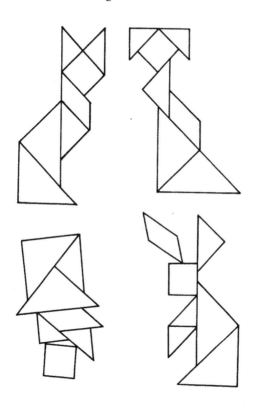

Charade

I-MAGI-NATION

Doublets

1 EEL
een
pen
pin
PIE

2 POOR
boor
book
rook
rock
rick
RICH

3 RAVEN
riven
risen
riser
MISER

4 OAT
rat
rot
roe
RYE

5 TREE
free
flee
fled
feed
weed
weld
wold
WOOD

6 GRASS
crass
cress
tress
trees
frees
freed
greed
GREEN

7 APE
are
ere
err
ear
mar
MAN

8 CAIN
chin
shin
spin
spun
spud
sped
aped
abed
ABEL

9 FLOUR
floor
flood
blood
brood
broad
BREAD

10 TEA
   sea
   set
   sot
   HOT

11 COMB
   come
   home
   hole
   hale
   hall
   hail
   HAIR

12 ROGUE
   vogue
   vague
   value
   valve
   halve
   heave
   helve
   leave
   lease
   least
   BEAST

13 ELM
   ell
   all
   ail
   air
   fir
   far
   oar
   OAK

14 ARMY
   arms
   aims
   dims
   dams
   dame
   name
   nave
   NAVY

15 BEANS
   beams
   seams
   shams
   shame
   shale
   shall
   shell
   SHELF

16 HOOK
   hoot
   host
   hist
   fist
   FISH

17 QUELL
   quill
   quilt
   guilt
   guile
   guide
   glide
   glade
   grade
   grave
   brave
   BRAVO

18 FURIES
   buries
   buried
   burked
   barked
   barred
   BARREL

19 BUY
bud
bid
aid
aim
arm
ark
ask
ASS

20 MINE
mint
mist
most
moat
coat
COAL

21 COSTS
posts
pests
tests
tents
tenth
tench
teach
peach
peace
PENCE

22 ONE
owe
ewe
eye
dye
doe
toe
too
TWO

23 BLUE
glue
glut
gout
pout
port
part
pant
pint
PINK

24 BLACK
blank
blink
clink
chink
chine
whine
WHITE

25 FISH
fist
gist
girt
gird
BIRD

Other titles introduced by Gyles Brandreth
from Notting Hill Editions*

On Christmas: A Seasonal Anthology
Introduced by Gyles Brandreth

This festive anthology offers an array of writers both old and new who have expressed their thoughts about Christmas with joy, nostalgia, grumpiness and wit.

Beautiful and Impossible Things: Selected Essays of Oscar Wilde
Introduced by Gyles Brandreth

Compiled from his lecture tours, newspaper articles, essays and epigrams, these writings showcase the varied aspects of Oscar Wilde's genius.

Break A Leg! A Dictionary of Theatrical Quotations
Compiled by Michèle Brown and Introduced by Gyles Brandreth

Gyles Brandreth introduces Michèle Brown, who has assembled a world-beating cast, including actors, dramatists, directors and even critics in this collection of wise and witty lines.

*All titles are available in the UK, and some titles are available in the rest of the world. For more information please visit www.nottinghilleditions.com.

A selection of our titles is distributed in the US and Canada by New York Review Books. For more information on available titles please visit www.nyrb.com.